WHAT'S YOUR MI[

**13 Ways to
Be "All In"**

Carrie Lightfoot Shappell

in Collaboration with Leah Shappell

Illustrated By: Luke Shappell

ELM HILL

A Division of
HarperCollins Christian Publishing

www.elmhillbooks.com

What's Your Ministry?
13 Ways to Be "All In"

Published in Nashville, Tennessee, by Elm Hill, an imprint of Thomas Nelson. Elm Hill and Thomas Nelson are registered trademarks of HarperCollins Christian Publishing, Inc.

Elm Hill titles may be purchased in bulk for educational, business, fund-raising, or sales promotional use. For information, please e-mail SpecialMarkets@ThomasNelson.com.

Library of Congress Cataloging-in-Publication Data

Library of Congress Control Number: 2019909404

ISBN 978-1-400327188 (Paperback)
ISBN 978-1-400327195 (eBook)

*This book is dedicated to my two grandmothers in Heaven,
who were amazing examples of faith and always believed in me.*

*And to my incredible husband, for loving me and our children so well and
for supporting all of my crazy adventures in this life!*

TABLE OF CONTENTS

INTRODUCTION

Colossians 3:23

"Whatever you do, work at it with all your heart, as working for the Lord, not for men."

I have lived what many would deem a charmed life. Dad was a teacher and a football coach. Mom stayed home with us for a few years and then joined my grandpa at his family-owned insurance agency. When I was nine, my parents built a house on family land, right by my grandparents and my aunt and uncle. Our church was across the field and eventually we would have a beach volleyball court, pool, and stone track all on what I now lovingly call our "compound." I grew up in a Christian home. My parents' foundation in their faith was, from my perspective, unshakeable. Everyone in my family has been actively involved in church. My mom has worked in music and youth ministries at many churches, while my dad has played drums on the praise team and has helped with youth ministries as well. My grandma Worman played the organ at Leo United Methodist Church for over fifty years, my grandpa Worman was a lay leader in the church and was involved with the Gideon ministry. Mammaw Lightfoot was a spiritual rock. She was a prayer warrior and I was always comforted after talking with her through life's challenges. Over the years, she volunteered to help many people in her church. Pappaw Lightfoot was an active member of several men's ministries at their church, Emerson Street Church of God in Missouri.

It's amazing to step back and realize how my family members filled so many different roles in my life. It truly was a village, and it was nice to have a village of believers. I have always been, and will always be, thankful for the family God chose for me. Because of my family's involvement, church wasn't an option, it just was. I don't remember ever questioning what we were doing Sunday morning or why. In fact, I remember going to prom and staying up until 5:00 a.m. on Sunday morning…guess where I was Sunday at 10:45 a.m.? Yep. And with my boyfriend, who now happens to be my husband.

My parents have been married for over forty years and both sets of grandparents made it at least fifty-five years before my grandmothers went to Heaven. Pretty impressive, right? I have a lot to live up to, but I look at it more like I have had amazing examples of how marriages work. This has been a wonderful blessing in my married life. My husband, Ben, and I have been married for nineteen years…and we look forward to the rest of our lives together. Fourteen years ago, we welcomed our first child, Luke, into the world and a little over two years later, he got to hold his baby sister, Leah. God has been good. He has always provided opportunities for us in our careers, in our community, and in our church. Oh, and did I mention that His plan was for us to live on the family "compound?" Yes, Ben and I now teach and coach in the high school that we both attended. It has been an awesome experience for us all and now our children get to grow up much like I did, with a support system that is beyond belief.

Why did I tell you all about my family and my life to start this book? For years I didn't think I had "a story." I have lived my life for Christ as best I could and have made mistakes and have fallen short many times. But life has been good to me. The most earth-shattering moments have been losing my grandmothers after strokes, but I had at least thirty years to enjoy my time with them and to learn from them here on Earth. There were some spiraling moments after losing one of my grandmothers, but the truth is I don't have a tragic story. My story includes many "God moments." It includes my basketball career, my family life, a movie that changed my perspective forever, and a career that has become a passion and has lent itself to living out my Christian beliefs and my "calling." In the parts of this story I want to share with you, I am hoping that you will gain insight into how God is working in you. Are you "all in?" What's your ministry?

Think About It....

Think about your story, the good parts and the bad. How does your story impact the way you live, the way you react, the things you feel?

What does "all in" mean to you? Would you consider yourself to be "all in" for God?

_____

Do you believe that you have a ministry? If so, what is your ministry?

_____

#1 REALIZE THAT EVERYONE HAS A STORY

Psalm 145:9

"The Lord is good to all; he has compassion on all he has made."

Everyone has a story. That story shapes how we see the world, how we react and respond in different situations. It affects how we choose our paths. I have spent a lot of my life thinking everyone had the same type of life as I had. Loving parents, amazing grandparents, and a spouse who is supportive beyond belief. I thought everyone wanted to and was encouraged to do their best and that doing the right thing was a priority. Boy, have my eyes been opened. And as my eyes continue to be opened, it seems odd that I had such a naive perspective for so long. Not everyone has the support system in place, positive moments to fall back on, or life goals that make them excited to get out of bed in the morning. We all have so many different stories. Within those stories are things we know about, or can find out about, and things that are hidden.

Colossians 3:12

"Therefore, as God's chosen people, holy and dearly loved, clothe yourselves with compassion, kindness, humility, gentleness, and patience."

The truth is that there are some parts of the story that we will never know about those around us. Sometimes that is because they don't want to share those with us. Sometimes it is simply because there are so many experiences we all have daily that there would be absolutely no way to know all of the pieces that come into play. In fact, we may not even always understand why *we* respond to certain situations the way we do. Lost in the shuffle of the craziness of life, we lose this truth. We operate on emotions instead of empathy. We make assumptions about intentions instead of remembering there are different perspectives. We burn bridges and, by doing this, we miss out on opportunities to be a light for Christ.

Ephesians 4:2

"Be completely humble and gentle; be patient, bearing with one another in love."

What if we operated our lives differently? What if we could, in every situation, think in multiple perspectives, realizing that not everyone thinks just like us because not everyone has lived the same life as us? I gave an assignment to a group of students recently to force them into thinking like another person (character). It was amazing what I learned from my students through this task. It was indeed an eye-opening experience. I asked them to think about the story of *Goldilocks and the Three Bears*. I then asked them to envision Goldilocks on trial. The task was to write a speech, from Baby Bear's perspective, that they would deliver to the jury. One student's response included a statement about Goldilocks being innocent. The student stated that Goldilocks was just hungry and tired because her parents couldn't afford to buy her food. This student was in fourth grade, and I can almost guarantee that the lack of food has been very real to him. No other student had thought of that as a reason for her innocence. I was thankful that he had found a safe way to communicate something that was very real and, just as importantly, I had been reminded that sometimes we learn that those around us have unexpected stories.

1 Peter 3:8

"Finally, all of you live in harmony with one another: be sympathetic, love as brothers, be compassionate and humble."

So how can we live differently? The most obvious way is to take time to get to know the people around you. Ask questions, listen well, and work on understanding. However, to get to know someone's entire story might be nearly impossible. What then? It is crucial that we assume the best intentions in people, or at the very least, understand that some part of their life has led them to a certain reaction or response. I don't think it is our job to try and comprehend every person's situation, but I do think that God wants us to show compassion, not anger or frustration toward others. As a teacher and coach, it took me a really long time to get to this. I tended to think that everyone had a hidden agenda, and if we are being honest there might be one in most situations. However, by just assuming that, I was causing a rift between me, my players, my students, and their parents. We were winning basketball games, I was teaching the game of basketball, students were finding success in the classroom, and there was a mutual respect, but I was constantly paranoid. It wasn't until I finally realized that everyone has a unique story, which forced me to begin looking at every situation from multiple perspectives, that I was able to break down those walls and allow God to work in all situations.

Romans 15:5

"May the God who gives endurance and encouragement give you a spirit of unity among yourselves as you follow Christ Jesus."

Activity: Think about those around you. What are their stories? Take time to learn about someone's story this week and challenge yourself to consider back-stories when you are responding to the words and reactions of those around you.

———————————————————

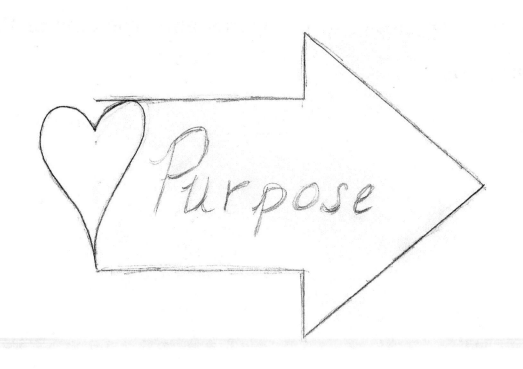

#2 Remember That We All Have a Purpose

Ephesians 2:10

"For we are God's workmanship, created in Christ Jesus to do good works, which God prepared in advance for us to do."

For a very long time, I thought it was just my personality. I needed to be needed. I found so much more in life if I was "in the game" and not "on the sidelines." Even if it was just to check off a silly to-do list, I needed to feel like I was getting things done for myself or other people. I wanted to feel purpose. To this day, I thrive on getting a checklist of things done for our family, and even sometimes take on a big project before Ben comes home from being out of town. I also sometimes sign up for leadership roles because, again, it is much more comfortable to be involved than to just sit back and watch. Then I started thinking about all of the books written about purpose and began to step back and observe how people around me respond when they feel needed...it is extremely evident that my family members, students, athletes, friends, and coworkers all thrive on being needed as well. The paths I take to find purpose may look different than others', but it still produces the same result. When I feel purpose I am at my best. And when I am at my best, I am making more of an impact for God.

Jeremiah 29:11

"For I know the plans I have for you," declares the LORD, "plans to prosper you and not to harm you, plans to give you hope and a future."

Our teenage son is a prime example of this. He has found purpose in running. While Luke has played lots of different sports over the years, running has been where he has found the most success. His entire demeanor changes during a running season. He becomes a better all-around athlete in other sports during this time and his confidence increases immensely. The key? He feels needed on the team. When people feel needed—feel that they have a purpose—they are happier, more successful, and they make a bigger impact. Purpose fosters perseverance and a confidence that is indescribable. I'll never forget the first time I watched Luke, who tends to be reserved, turn to shake hands with another runner or run around the cross country course to cheer on his teammates. It made my heart happy to see how his newfound confidence was already changing his behaviors in a way that would allow him to impact others.

Another person who comes to mind is Coach Barnett. He is a person whom I have a deep respect for as a coach. The reason is simple. While I believe that Coach Barnett has an understanding of the skills and strategies needed in the sports he has coached, *how* he is living out purpose by being an inspiring coach has a great impact on the players. Both my son and daughter have played for this outstanding coach. Every player on his team always feels that he or she is important, they feel appreciated. When you are watching him coach, you would never know who the best player is or who the worst player is on the team. Coach Barnett treats them all the same, with an encouragement and positive motivation that is second to none. In a world where players feel so much pressure to be perfect, he makes them feel needed always, even when they are struggling. I'm inspired by how he coaches each and every team member. This is how God feels about us; He loves each of us the same, truly wants us all to find success, and is cheering us on every step of the way. We just need to have faith that we can find purpose in every situation He allows us to experience.

Romans 8:28–29

"And we know that in all things God works for the good of those who love him, who have been called according to his purpose. For those God foreknew he also predestined to be conformed to the image of his Son, that he might be the firstborn among many brothers."

My point? Find where you are needed in every situation and go with it, enjoy the ride, and then maybe your impact will help others find purpose as well. Be "all in" and by your actions and words, give others a reason to be "all in." Your "ministry" doesn't have to be one big thing. It can be lots of little things in lots of little ways. The pieces of the puzzle that God has designed in you, His masterpiece. I heard it said by our minister once that we spend so much time trying to find our one purpose or destination that we miss opportunities where we are right now. It's so true. God has His hand in everything you do and He has purpose(s) for you...that's why you are here. If you are struggling through not feeling needed, know that God needs you to show His light or love to others, give people hope, help build His kingdom, and make this world a better place.

Psalm 139:14

"I praise you because I am fearfully and wonderfully made; your works are wonderful, I know that full well."

What if we consistently reminded ourselves that God needs us? What if we continually served His people, led a life pleasing to Him so that others would want to be a part of this, and what if we simply helped give people hope by what we said and how we lived? We wouldn't need earthly things to help us feel needed, but we would find purpose daily because we would be living out God's love. In the end, we need God and He needs us to be His hands and feet on Earth. The most important purposes in this life are found in this truth.

Proverbs 19:21

"Many are the plans in a man's heart, but it is the Lord's purpose that prevails."

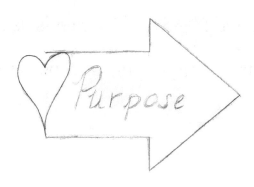

Activity: Where is God leading you? Where do you feel needed? Pay attention. When opportunities arise this week, write them down and pray about them. Sometimes the opportunities that seem trivial make the biggest impact and provide meaningful moments for others.

————————————————————

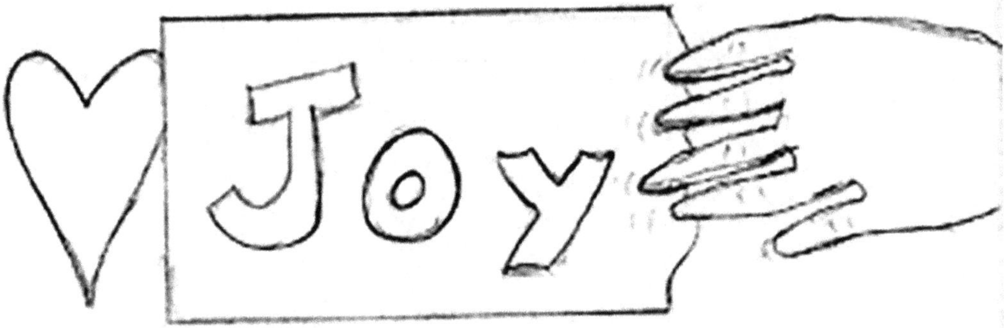
Joy

#3 FIGURE OUT WHAT IS STEALING YOUR JOY

Galatians 5: 22–23

"But the fruit of the Spirit is love, joy, peace, patience, kindness, goodness, faithfulness, gentleness and self-control. Against such things there is no law."

For years, I dehumanized my opponents—anyone who didn't agree with me or anyone who competed against me. I figured it was easier to do that than to just let my guard down and show grace. I'm not wired for conflict or bitterness to live in me or be part of my daily routine, especially when it comes to relationships with people, so this practice began to steal my joy. Amazing what God shows us as we grow in Him and when we are put to the test. After many years, I finally realized that this wasn't worth it, I had absolutely nothing to prove, and that I only really had control over a few things. One of those being my attitude—the choice of how to respond to the things I can't control. Oh, how I wish I would've figured this out so much earlier in my career as a coach and teacher.

James 1: 2–3

"Consider it pure joy, my brothers, whenever you face trials of many kinds, because you know that the testing of your faith develops perseverance."

Sometimes when we put that wall up, our ministry becomes counterproductive. While I may have had an impact on the people who agreed with me or were on "my team," God's grace was not shown to my "enemies." And isn't that who we are called to minister to most? In fact, doesn't true character really show when we are faced with adversity? Looking back, I missed so many opportunities and when I finally faced adversity with conviction and grace, lives were changed. True joy was found.

Romans 5:1–5

"Therefore, since we have been justified through faith, we have peace with God through our Lord Jesus Christ, through whom we have gained access by faith into this grace in which we now stand. And we rejoice in the hope of the glory of God. Not only so, but we also rejoice in our sufferings, because we know that suffering produces perseverance; perseverance, character; and character, hope. And hope does not disappoint us, because God has poured out his love into our hearts by the Holy Spirit, whom he has given us."

Why did it take me so long to figure that out? Pride. Distrust. Loss of perspective or a lack there of. So what happened? When my team lost, I was miserable. When someone disagreed with me in a harsh way, I was disheartened and would shut them out. When something or someone caused controversy, I dwelled on it and worried about it. As these began to build up in my life, I became more negative, had a hard time focusing on the good things in my life, and probably wasn't the most pleasant person to be around. I never once reminded myself to just trust God until it was extreme and I had a meltdown. Yet, in the middle of these meltdown moments, it still took me too long to fall to my knees. It was like, "I got this God, I'm in control...but if I need you to save me in the end I will let you know."

1 Peter 1: 8–9

"Though you have not seen him, you love him; and even though you do not see him now, you believe in him and are filled with an inexpressible and glorious joy, for you are receiving the goal of your faith, the salvation of your souls."

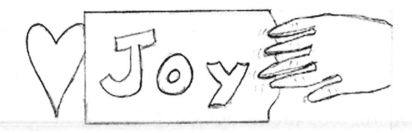

I was certain I was in control. Let's think about that for a minute. I was "in control" of other people and their actions and didn't need God to intervene in situations that were causing me stress? Saying that I actually felt this way makes me cringe. I was allowing these people and situations to steal my joy, preoccupied by frustration and negativity. What happened because of this was so unfortunate. When I should've been happy about something, I couldn't fully rejoice because I was so worried about what I needed to control that wasn't going well. I might have had a smile on my face and given lots of hugs—I masked it well—but it wasn't 100 percent joy. That is an exhausting life. Overcome the obstacles that are stealing your joy…it is liberating and it is what God wants! When you choose joy because of the life you have in Him, others see this, want to know how they can find it, and lives are changed, including yours.

Psalm 16:11

"You have made known to me the path of life; you will fill me with joy in your presence, with eternal pleasures at your right hand."

Activity: Think about something in your life that is stealing your joy. Break down that wall. Physically write it down and physically destroy it. Get rid of it and move forward with God at your side.

—————————————————————

#4 Focus on What It Is Really About

Romans 12:9–10

"Love must be sincere. Hate what is evil; cling to what is good. Be devoted to one another in brotherly love. Honor one another above yourselves."

In a word, relationships. It's overlooked really. We choose success, media, technology, etc. … over relationships and it's only getting worse. How many times have you thought, as you walked by someone, "I really don't have time to ask how he or she is doing, but I should." What choice did you make? Walk by and give a quick hello on your way through, or did you ask? I'm a talker, so asking that question comes pretty naturally. But as life has sped up and my career has gotten busier, I have had to make an effort to slow down and ask. I have learned that building relationships is critical to how we impact this world. It is the best avenue to truly building God's kingdom.

1 Thessalonians 5:11

"Therefore encourage one another and build each other up, just as in fact you are doing."

It's important and becoming more important in this generation. With the influence of social media, technology, and all of the negative effects we are seeing, our commitment to developing real relationships is necessary. I've benefited many times from people taking time to ask me how I am doing. I call them my angel moments. I have had a lot of angel moments in this life. They have come in many different forms of people. My God is amazing! My ministry is coaching, teaching, being a mom, being a wife, and being a friend. In every one of these, it is critical to build relationships and show I care. Not for selfish reasons, but because that's what I believe God wants us to do. It's what I believe Jesus was all about when He was here on Earth.

Hebrews 13:16

"And do not forget to do good and to share with others, for with such sacrifices God is pleased."

Jesus offered friendship to the rich, the poor, the healthy, the sick, the bold, the meek, his friends, and even his enemies. When you offer a healthy and positive relationship to someone, it can be life-changing. You could be the last hope, you could be the first one who cared enough, or you could simply be a ray of sunshine in a dreary moment. Regardless, you will make a difference. It doesn't matter whether a person is two days old or 102 years old, we need each other. That makes the pursuit of taking time to ask how others are doing, in order to show you care, even more critical.

John 15:12

"My command is this: Love each other as I have loved you."

I've worked in many different situations as an educator. I've been around elementary students and teachers, middle school students and teachers, high school athletes and coaches, alternative school students, and many different administrators. In every one of my career experiences, positive relationships have always been a key element to the success of the students, athletes, teachers, coaches, schools, and the district. I made the argument earlier that the power of relationships is overlooked. I think we miss so many opportunities when we forget the importance of this. How do we build these relationships? We show that we care. We ask questions, we show interest in the answers, we listen to questions and concerns, we show up in the good times and in the bad. We live like Jesus did.

1 Corinthians 13:4–7

"Love is patient, love is kind. It does not envy, it does not boast, it is not proud. It is not rude, it is not self-seeking, it is not easily angered, it keeps no record of wrongs. Love does not delight in evil but rejoices with the truth. It always protects, always trusts, always hopes, always perseveres."

Activity: Make a list of things that are pulling you away from building relationships (both with people you know and people you don't know). Beside each one, write a resolution to do better, even if it's a small change. Small steps make great impact possible.

———————————————————

#5 EMBRACE GUARDIAN ANGELS AND GOD MOMENTS

James 1:17

"Every good and perfect gift is from above, coming down from the Father of the heavenly lights, who does not change like shifting shadows."

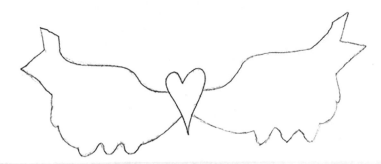

I do believe that God gifted me a strong faith in Him from a very early age and my family continued to build that through our involvement in church. However, it wasn't until I was in high school and college that I realized completely that people in my life were not placed there by chance and, conversely, I wasn't placed in their lives by chance either. It is all part of God's amazing plan; my family, my colleagues, my friends, my mentors, my students, my athletes, and even those I have brief moments with in this life. Amazing blessings have happened because of these people and I have been so fortunate to realize these blessings in my life almost daily.

Philippians 4:7

"And the peace of God, which transcends all understanding, will guard your hearts and your minds in Christ Jesus."

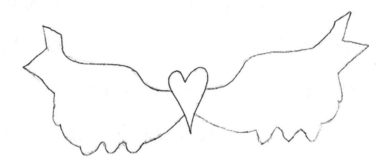

Think about all that "falls in line" for your life to be in existence and to be where you are now. Next, think about what "fell in line" for you to meet your closest friends or your spouse, have your kids or land the job you wanted or needed. Finally, think about the windy road you've taken to work with those you work with and those random people you've met at some point and conversed with... never really seems like coincidence to me. All of the things that "fell in line" were God moments. It's all part of His plan for you. I consider anyone who has touched my life in a positive way, and have therefore revealed God's work, a Guardian Angel. These angels take many forms. From my two grandmothers to a man I met one time and talked to for an hour in a hotel lobby, to my husband, to my best girl friend, to my kids, and so many others. I am thankful for each that God has and will continue to place in my path.

Psalm 91:11–12

"For he will command his angels concerning you to guard you in all your ways; they will lift you up in their hands, so that you will not strike your foot against a stone."

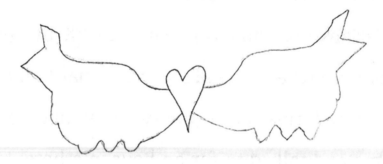

Grandma Marna Jo guarded me from negativity...well she did her best. I spent so much time with her from the time I was nine until the day she entered Heaven. She always told the other side of the story, always had something kind to say, and was always smiling. She truly looked at the world through God's eyes. My Mammaw was a person whom I saw only about four times a year but she was my prayer warrior. She was the one I called when times were tough and I needed encouragement. She guarded me from losing hope, because she knew God could handle anything I was going through. Anthony, a college basketball coach of a team we were facing, was a surprise in my life. He walked by me in a hotel lobby as I was writing a college paper and listening to my headphones. I still don't have a clue why he felt compelled to stop and talk, but his timing was perfect (well, God's timing was perfect). What Anthony said to me in that hour was so incredibly powerful that it became part of my testimony. He guarded me from bitterness. It's funny and wonderful how God works.

Philippians 4:19

"And my God will meet all your needs according to his glorious riches in Christ Jesus."

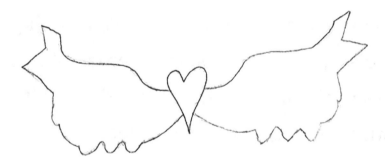

Ben Shappell has guarded me from being anxious. I'm definitely not making an argument that I am laid back in any way shape or form, but he is in my life to keep me calm, among many other reasons. God knew completely that I needed someone to calm my fears and love me through them. Ben has done that so very well. Kayla started coaching with me under an unusual chain of events. Coaching together led us to an amazing friendship. When my life was spiraling a bit, she guarded me from temptation. Kayla has been so brutally honest with me in times where that was exactly what I needed and continues to never place judgment on my shortcomings. Luke guards me from losing perspective and Leah guards me from taking myself too seriously. And there have been so many others. Don't get me wrong: all of these things that my "angels" have guarded me from can still be a struggle, but I share all of these examples because God knows what we need and when we need it. He provides God Moments and Guardian Angels perfectly. He knows who we need in our life and He delivers. Every. Single. Time. Be aware of God Moments and Guardian Angels in your life. Listen when God speaks through those around you and through events you experience.

Philippians 1:3–6

"I thank my God every time I remember you. In all my prayers for all of you, I always pray with joy because of your partnership in the gospel from the first day until now, being confident of this, that he who began a good work in you will carry it on to completion until the day of Christ Jesus."

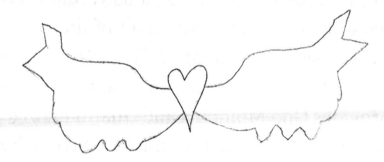

Activity: Write and send three thank-you notes or notes of encouragement to someone who you consider a Guardian Angel or someone who you have experienced a God Moment with.

———————————————

#6 Survive Outside Your Comfort Zone

Mark 1:16–20

"As Jesus walked beside the Sea of Galilee, he saw Simon and his brother Andrew casting a net into the lake, for they were fishermen. 'Come, follow me,' Jesus said, 'and I will make you fishers of men.' At once they left their nets and followed Him. When he had gone a little farther, he saw James son of Zebedee and his brother John in a boat, preparing their nets. Without delay he called them, and they left their father Zebedee in the boat with the hired men and followed him."

Your comfort zone is the place you like to "live." It's the place you feel at home. It's the events you like to attend. It's the activities you feel confident participating in. The problem is that if all you ever focus on is what is comfortable, you may never realize what all you are capable of and how much of an impact you could have. I can't imagine how the disciples felt when they were called out of their current lives into a life literally walking with Jesus Christ…talk about outside your comfort zone. They walked away from everything for a man they had only just met. Can you imagine that? I can't…but I can't imagine if they hadn't either. So many things would be different. They wouldn't ever have made the impact they did on the entire future of society.

Joshua 1:9

"Have I not commanded you? Be strong and courageous. Do not be terrified; do not be discouraged, for the LORD your God will be with you wherever you go."

In Building 429's song "Impossible," they claim that when we rise above what the earth has to offer and rely on God, nothing is impossible. This song talks about trusting God in everything. If we are able to do this, why don't we venture outside of our comfort zones? Why don't we invite a friend to church? Why don't we walk the walk or talk about our walk with Christ more? Why don't we try something new? Why do we care so much about what others think? Why do we hide our feelings and beliefs? Why don't we take risks?

Philippians 4:13

"I can do everything through him who gives me strength."

The first time I can remember being outside my comfort zone was playing basketball at the University of Rhode Island. I was far away from family for the first time in my life, living with two teammates I had just met, and experiencing some uncomfortable situations. I had to grow up so much in a short period of time. He never left my side, I experienced so many God moments, and I learned how to find strength in His word every day. I am certain that I was more aware of how God was working in my life during that time period because I was so reliant on Him. That, friends, is what being outside your comfort zone forces you to do.

2 Timothy 1:7

"For God did not give us a spirit of timidity, but a spirit of power, of love and of self-discipline."

My comfort zone has changed drastically over the last few years in a new position at work. I've always been a talker, so presenting to more people hasn't been a problem. However, the first year of my new job wasn't the easiest. It required cold calls to businesses to request field trip opportunities, advocating for a population of students who needed more attention (with advocacy comes frustration), and implementation of a new program in which my new colleagues were not completely confident in yet. My comfort zone includes peace and no conflict. So you can imagine that the first few times I heard the word "no," the first few times that teachers looked at me with apprehension, and the first few times I was questioned were painful.

I was a bit unsettled, as I still was unsure I had made the right decision by leaving the classroom…a place I dearly loved and missed. But I held tight to the truth that God had put this in my life and there was a reason. I began to look for my God moments and it is interesting how much more receptive we are of those when we are outside our comfort zone. I found them.

Ecclesiastes 3:1

"There is a time for everything, and a season for every activity under heaven."

Activity: Try something new, outside your comfort zone, this week and tell others about it. Encourage them to try something outside of their comfort zone too. Also, pray that God will open your eyes to an opportunity to share your faith or testimony with someone or invite someone to church. Sharing your faith with someone can be a bit of a risk, but it is *always* worth it.

———————————————————

#7 Create a Soundtrack of Your Life

1 Timothy 4:12

"Don't let anyone look down on you because you are young, but set an example for the believers in speech, in life, in love, in faith and in purity."

Do you have a theme song? Or a few songs in your life that were relevant at different stages you were in? You know, those songs that you would walk down the road to if your life was made into a movie? Yeah, I think about that kind of stuff. Music is one of my vices. That and cherry coke…that's as rebellious as I get, folks. Anyway, back to my soundtrack. It actually didn't take me that long to come up with this soundtrack, as I have had many different theme songs for the many stages in my life. When I began writing this book, there was a song that was very relevant. It was Newsboy's "Live with Abandon." So what does that say about me? It actually says many things, but most importantly it confirms my commitment to giving my life to Christ 100 percent no matter where I am and what stage of life I am in. Living with abandon to me means living out life full speed with no regrets, but not just this worldly life. A life filled with Christ and one in which others will see Christ through me. I want to live a life in which I can be me and through being me, others want to know why I am so happy, upbeat, faithful, loyal, and hopeful.

Romans 15:13

"May the God of hope fill you with all joy and peace as you trust in him, so that you may overflow with hope by the power of the Holy Spirit."

Two other songs that would make the soundtrack would be "Thrive" by Casting Crowns and, more recently, "joy." by King and Country. In "Thrive," we are reminded that anything is possible when we find joy, faith, and love through Jesus Christ. So many times I am around people who are so sad. Now, as I have said, my life has been a cakewalk compared to many others. I am not advocating that every person has to be happy all of the time. Even in this charmed life, I have not accomplished that. And when I say sadness, I'm not talking about the kind of sadness that comes with death, defeat, and illness. I am talking about internal sadness and negativity that is difficult to overcome. I am talking about not being able to find faith that God will bring you through life's storms. I would contend that we have all gone down this path of sadness and negativity before. It is hard not to, and when the chips aren't falling right, Satan is ready to intervene. Satan wants us to be sad eternally and question God. There are things that happen on this earth that we will never understand, but God is good and we have to try and find hope and love through it all while encouraging others do to the same through Him. I am talking about the outlook on life in which we believe that life is good, people are good, and through death, defeat, and illness God will carry us. He loves us unconditionally and if we truly rely on Him, He will give us joy, renew our faith, and heal our hearts through all trials. The song "joy." challenges us to get up every morning and live life well no matter what it throws our way, choosing to find joy!

2 Thessalonians 3:5

"May the Lord direct your hearts into God's love and Christ's perseverance."

What are some other tracks that would make my soundtrack? It would include the following songs for different stages of life: "Jesus Freak" by DC Talk, "Seize the Day" from the musical *Newsies*, "Fly Like an Eagle" by Seal, "A Spoonful of Sugar" from Mary Poppins, "All My Life" by K-Ci & JoJo, "Do Something" by Matthew West, "Fix My Eyes" by for KING & COUNTRY , "Have It All" by Jason Mraz, and "Look Up Child" by Lauren Daigle. There are so many more and this list could grow daily. It is really fun to walk down the hall, or the street, and envision walking to the beat of these songs or the intention of their lyrics. But, more importantly, the lyrics of these songs are meaningful and listening to these helps remind me of how I have lived and how I want to live. Sharing God's love with those around me, wishing the best for everyone, finding joy, and persevering by trusting that He is by my side every step of the way.

Matthew 5:14–16

"You are the light of the world. A city on a hill cannot be hidden. Neither do people light a lamp and put it under a bowl. Instead they put it on its stand, and it gives light to everyone in the house. In the same way, let your light shine before men, that they may see your good deeds and praise your Father in Heaven."

I WANT TO LIVE WITH ABANDON. After losing my grandmother a few years ago, I realize that now more than ever I need to live out this life to the best of my ability and NOT wait. Life is too short. It is too short to not give 100 percent all of the time. It is imperative that we live with hope, stay optimistic, try new things, put ourselves out there, take risks, have fun, enjoy life, and most importantly live with abandon doing all of this for God... knowing that this is short-lived and everything we do should be in His honor and to build His kingdom!

Colossians 3:17

"And whatever you do, whether in word or deed, do it all in the name of the Lord Jesus, giving thanks to God the Father through him."

Activity: Create a soundtrack of your life, or at least of the last few years. Make a playlist of these songs and listen to them to remind you of memories and meaning. Share them with someone else and tell part of your story through music. Oh, and sometimes, just for fun, walk down the street to a song, pretending you are starring in a movie about your life.

_____

INTERMISSION

Hebrews 10:36

"You need to persevere so that when you have done the will of God, you will receive what he has promised."

Derailed:

For Christians, there are many moments that don't make sense. What we believe to be the perfect plan for us often gets what I call "derailed." It's like we are chugging along and everything is going wonderfully and all of the sudden, we are off the track—our track, that is. But we have to trust in God, that His plan might "derail" us, and there might be hidden blessings. We have to remember to be open to these blessings in the moments that seem confusing and unsettling.

When I was about sixteen years old, I started getting recruitment letters from basketball coaches around the Midwest and soon I was receiving letters from colleges around the country. My parents and I had several conversations about what I wanted to be "when I grew up" and if in fact my future plans involved college basketball. I loved basketball and also really liked the idea of a free education while playing a game I loved, but I also felt tugged into the ministry. I was "all in" in basketball, and was very intentional about using my high school basketball career to tell others about God, but this tug had me feeling like I still needed to do more for God. I had a female minister at the time and had much respect and admiration for her and her leadership in our church. I had always been very strong in my faith and truly enjoyed working with the children in our church. I was pretty sure church ministry was where I was headed. This was no surprise to many people. In fact, one of my coaches at a basketball camp, and now a close friend, Eddie, once said, "Lightfoot (my maiden name), you are always trying to change the world." He still says that to me sometimes when I am working through difficult matters as a coach. So where did that leave me? Soon I would receive contact from the University of Evansville, a Methodist university and a place that I could major in theology in order to follow that tug into ministry. I had visited a few schools and the University of Evansville seemed like the perfect fit. In the summer before my senior year, the coaches told me that once they saw me play at camp, they were going to offer me a scholarship...everything was going as planned—well, as I planned. We know how God works though, right? About two weeks before the camp they would see me play at, I was hospitalized for appendicitis and had an emergency appendectomy. That put me out for four weeks. Heartbreaking for me, as I was ready to commit immediately and have my decision out of the way. I was impatient and I totally had this whole plan figured out. But it needed to happen NOW!

After calling my friend Eddie, we found a camp that I could attend in Ohio instead, once my recovery time was completed. I called the coaches from the University of Evansville to let them know and they said they would have to wait to see me play until my school season because they had other travel plans that weekend. My parents and I made the decision to attend this camp anyway, and after two games, I had a full scholarship offer from the University of Rhode Island. This was a school I hadn't even talked to before this camp. I visited Rhode Island and signed right before my senior season began, with intention to now major in psychology and education. That was the first ministry tug and dream that I wanted to happen RIGHT NOW that got derailed.

Think About It....

Have you ever felt a "tug" from God? What did you do about it?

_____

Have you ever experienced your plan being derailed?

_____

When your plans get derailed, how do you respond? How should we respond?

_____

Matthew 6:10

"Your kingdom come, your will be done, as earth as it is in heaven."

Four months:

So my impatience took over and I was set to attend a school that was thirteen hours from my family. I'm still not convinced that my decision was made for the right reasons (mostly because of my impatience), but God had it all under control and I was ready to go. "All in" with His plans for me and college basketball. In fact, one thing that I was convinced of was that for some unknown reason, He did not have plans for me to attend the University of Evansville. I didn't understand, but I had faith and I believed that when one door closed, God opened a window somewhere else. I settled into the fact that if I majored in psychology, I could use it to be a Christian counselor. Education would just be icing on the cake and another avenue I could pursue with my degree. I came from a family of educators as well, so I knew that it was a great mission and rewarding career. Too many God moments in the four months I was at University of Rhode Island to discuss in detail, but it was "just me and God" for those four months. Through homesickness, finding and attending a new church, dealing with the ups and downs of college basketball or life, and lastly through a knee surgery, I was now more reliant on God than I had ever been. I saw family members about once a month and there was a countdown for sure, but I grew closer to God in those four months than in any year of my life. Think about that, four months. I wasn't a theology major, I had no plans to be a minister, and I was now more connected to God because my plans had been derailed.

Ironic, isn't it? Proof that God meets us where we are. But at the end of that four months and after my knee surgery put me on the sidelines, the homesickness got worse. I finished the semester and decided to transfer closer to home. The amazing part to the end of my story at Rhode Island was how many of my teammates were sad to see me go and told me how much I had meant in their lives. I had no idea and here's the thing...I wasn't trying. I was very focused on my life with Christ, but I didn't take a lot of time to build relationships. I really only had one or two teammates that I became close to. I studied hard, practiced and played basketball with commitment, and worked on my faith. I was, as I have always been, trying to live for God and set an example for Him, but I didn't preach to others. I didn't try to push my beliefs on others, I really just lived for Him. In doing so, I found that others noticed the strength my faith provided in the face of adversity. Sometimes intentionally living for God *is* the best form of ministering we can provide. Example alone. Not by being perfect, but by focusing on faith and being genuine …being real! In fact, my guess is that if I would've tried to push my faith by words, it would've been rejected by a few of my teammates. Being genuine and real, not perfect, is how we best represent Christianity.

I was set to visit three universities within three hours of my hometown and after my first visit, and with another scholarship offered beginning in January, I committed to Indiana University-Purdue University at Indianapolis (IUPUI). I was going to finish my career as a Jaguar. I felt at home and knew a few of the players already from playing basketball with or against them in the summers. It was, in my mind, the "perfect fit," but remember that even the "perfect fit" has moments of challenge. The first challenge for me at IUPUI: you cannot major in psychology and education, so pick one. I chose education, a decision I will never regret and a decision that I believe led me into my "ministry."

Think About It...

Has there ever been a time in your life that you felt closer to God?

_____

Has God ever taken a "derailed" situation and made the best of it with you?

_____

In what ways are you ministering every day? In what ways could you?

_____

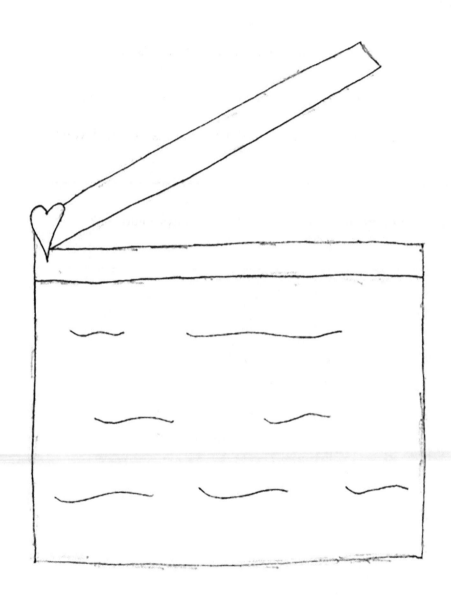

#8 LEARN LESSONS ON LIFE AT THE MOVIES

Proverbs 18:15

"The heart of the discerning acquires knowledge, the ears of the wise seek it out."

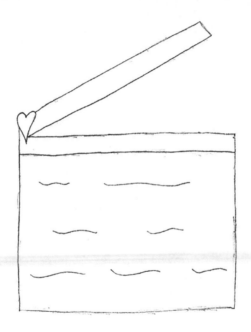

I am one of those people who have a hard time separating life from a movie they're watching. My movies, therefore, are usually those that have a happy ending. Basically I watch Disney movies, a chick flick, a sports movie, or a Christian film. Every once in a while I watch a movie that is "outside the box" for me. It seems like I always learn something from these movies....

Proverbs 2:6

"For the Lord gives wisdom, and from his mouth come knowledge and understanding."

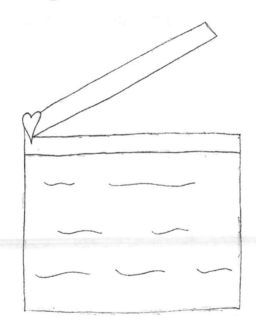

While on a flight recently, I watched the movie *Before I Fall*. A really sad movie, but since I struggle to keep movies separate from life, of course I thought about what can be learned from the movie. In short, the film is about a girl who relives the day she and her friends are in a car accident (and die) over and over again. Through the movie, she tries living the day differently…many different ways to change this story, but she continues to wake up to the previous morning. She finally realizes her fate and what she must do. I don't want to ruin the movie for you, but in essence she realizes that before she "falls" she wants, and actually needs, to make a difference in the lives of her friends and family. That definitely got me thinking.

Acts 20:24

"However, I consider my life worth nothing to me, if only I may finish the race and complete the task the Lord Jesus has given me-the task of testifying to the gospel of God's grace."

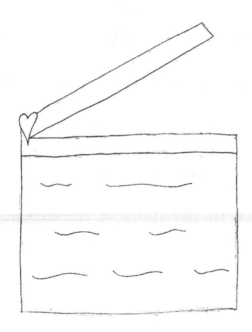

What if we lived every day as if it were our last? Not to be sad about it, but to realize that there are things we would like to do before it all ends...for God and the good of everyone we come into contact with. This isn't a challenge to check off our bucket list items or to accomplish something great in one day. It's a challenge to think about the legacy we leave behind that someone else might want to continue. It's a challenge to make the lives of others around us bearable, and maybe even enjoyable. It's a challenge to leave that legacy of God's love. This seems like an easy thing to do, right?

2 Timothy 4:7

"I have fought the good fight, I have finished the race, I have kept the faith."

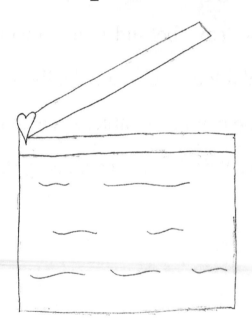

Can you stand up to someone who is doing wrong? Can you stop gossiping about others? Can you be just as happy and encouraging when someone else wins or succeeds? I challenge you to rethink how you live every day and what you might do differently if you knew you didn't have much more time on earth to make a difference. Not to earn your way into Heaven, but to simply be a light to someone else and for Christ. Not to win a reward, but to make someone smile. Not only to find blessings in your life, but to bless someone else and be intentional about that.

Philippians 4:8

"Finally, brothers, whatever is true, whatever is noble, whatever is right, whatever is pure, whatever is lovely, whatever is admirable-if anything is excellent or praiseworthy-think about these things."

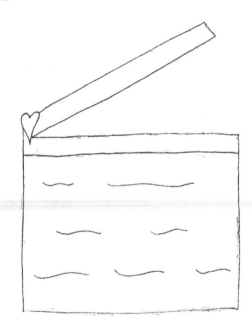

Activity: Make a list of things you want to do and ways you want to impact ... don't put it off! Get going!

————————————————————

#9 Live Life for and with God

Galatians 1:10

"Am I now trying to win the approval of man, or of God? Or am I trying to please men? If I were still trying to please men, I would not be a servant of Christ."

After I held my grandmother's hand as she left our world to enter Heaven, I had some questions to answer. Through some moments of spiraling, mistakes made, and definite moments in which I didn't feel like myself, I think I truly and finally found some answers. How in the world does that happen? After witnessing the fragility of life, I realized that life wasn't about living out everyone else's expectations, it was about living out God's expectations ... knowing there is a definite intersection sometimes. For example, my parents had expectations in our household. Many of those were in direct agreement with the teachings we learned in the Bible. However, I felt as if I had always done what people expected me to do. And that maybe that wasn't always what I wanted to do or even what God wanted me to do.

Proverbs 3: 5–6

"Trust in the Lord with all your heart and lean not on your own understanding; in all your ways acknowledge him, and he will make your paths straight."

No regrets, though. I never gave into a negative peer pressure and in fact, it was the exact opposite. I almost always did what everyone thought I should do, call it a healthy fear of disappointing someone. Fast forward into my children playing youth sports. Those low moments that they or we have experienced? Those seem bigger when you are living out the expectations you feel others have for you. A friend of mine once called it the "fish bowl mentality." You feel like everyone is watching your successes and failures. Change your perspective. It's not about those people. God gave me the physical and mental health to participate in sports. God gave me that and then followed it with opportunities to be a coach, a mentor. Competing is part of the process, but winning to God looks different from winning to us and those around us.

Psalm 119:105

"Your word is a lamp to my feet and a light for my path."

In God's eyes, trying our best with the gifts He's given us is sufficient. Being a good example of His love and grace during the course of our lives with family, friends, coworkers, teammates, coaches, players, supervisors, and opponents is enough. Doing these things and remembering to be thankful for the life and blessings He has given us is our gift back. Striking out, missing a shot, losing a race, not getting a job, giving into temptation...those are all "failures" in this life and most of the time feel larger than life because of others' opinions and expectations. In God's eyes a bigger picture exists and those "failures" are building blocks. The way we respond is what matters to Him.

1 Corinthians 12:5–6

"There are different kinds of service, but the same Lord. There are different kinds of working, but the same God works all of them in all men."

I recently was watching a regional championship game that my husband was coaching. I mentioned that I had said a prayer going into the last inning and someone said, "Do you really think God cares about high school sports?" That made me pause for a moment and think, but I still believe He does. I don't think He cares about us meeting others' expectations and winning all of the time, but I do believe that through high school sports, He provides a platform to witness. God's hope is that we use that platform so that others may find faith and feel His love like we do. If you ever get a chance to listen to Matthew West's song "Do Something," listen closely to the lyrics. God uses us to be His hands and feet, it is His expectations that matter most. My mantra? Live for God, surprise people every now and then by doing the unexpected, and be aware of whose expectations I am trying to live out.

2 Corinthians 5:9

"So we make it our goal to please him, whether we are at home in the body or away from it."

Activity: Make a collage of things that make you and God happy.

—————————————————

#10 Fail Well

Psalm 73:26

"My flesh and my heart may fail, but God is the strength of my heart and my portion forever."

For years, I have failed at failing…weird statement, right? Well when you are a competitive person, it is really difficult to lose or fail. However, there are more definitions to "failing" than just losing on the scoreboard. You can "fail" during an argument about something you feel very strongly about, you can feel "failure" when someone chooses to walk away from you, or you can feel a loss of hope because things have changed and how you think they should be may not ever happen again…"failure." In all of the above, I have struggled. In fact, I have struggled more when failing in those less obvious ways than when losing on the scoreboard. That's hard to believe…trust me! You would have to see me coach a basketball game.

Romans 12:15

"Rejoice with those who rejoice. Mourn with those who mourn."

Why do I fail at failing? Sometimes it is because I am over-the-top passionate, and sometimes it is because I'm stubborn. God calls us to be able to see other perspectives. He also expects us to celebrate when others have success. That's convicting. Because I truly feel that God gave me my passionate personality, I have a hard time believing He wants me to just sit back and let everyone else "win" or push their opinions or agendas onto me. I believe, though, that when I do fail, He wants me to fail well…gracefully, lovingly, and with a side order of humility.

James 4:10

"Humble yourselves before the Lord, and he will lift you up."

So what does that look like? For the last few years as a coach, I have challenged my players to focus on encouraging someone else in times of frustration. For example, if you missed your last three shots, make an effort to give someone else a high five during a dead ball and say "Let's go," "Keep it up," or "Good job." I truly believe that if we focus our energy on encouraging those around us, we lose focus on our failures and are able to find joy even in these moments. This doesn't mean I do this well, but when I do, it is a game changer. It took me fourteen years to figure this out as a coach and it is still a work in progress for me as a parent.

Philippians 2:3

"Do nothing out of selfish ambition or vain conceit, but in humility consider others better than yourselves."

My Luke is a multisport athlete and in basketball he plays his role pretty well. He is not flashy and doesn't really look to shoot. His confidence is a work in progress, but he rebounds well, plays good defense, and knows the game…he has grown up in the gym since birth.

There was a game in junior high that I will never forget. We were in a close game and Luke was in at the end. This was a bit unusual. He had several key rebounds, played great defense, and even had a put-back at the right time to help his team build the lead. I was, of course, a nervous wreck but afterwards so proud of his effort and so excited that they had won. Being a coach at his school (our school is a seventh to twelfth building), I keep myself separate from other parents and fans. I probably look antisocial, but really I just need separation. Anyway, that night I watched as he entered the gym after the game. Two other dads, whose sons had not had as much success on that given night, went out of their way to find Luke, give him a high five, and tell him how awesome he played. Talk about humbling. I'm sure those dads have no idea how much that meant to Luke and me, but I am so thankful for the lesson God taught me in that moment. I use to think that if I or my family members "failed" and I was happy for those who succeeded as a result, that was an admittance of giving up. And if we are being honest, I was so jealous. Being happy for someone else's success when we fail isn't quitting. It's realizing that this life is about "failing well" and understanding that people will see God through our attitudes in those moments.

My Leah has a beautiful heart. As early as preschool, she began taking care of everyone around her. She spends as much time as she can doing things for others and cheering on anyone she knows, or doesn't know. Leah was going through a struggling season of hitting in softball and she had this great hit to the outfield. It was in the air and a younger player who was subbing for the other team caught it. She was a little bummed but still had a smile on her face. After the game, I expressed how proud I was of her hit and told her it was a bummer it was caught. Leah's response? "Mom, I was so happy that she caught it. I bet she felt really good about that." A lesson for us all—choose joy, and be happy for others, even in our "failures."

1 Thessalonians 5:16–18

"Be joyful always, pray continually; give thanks in all circumstances, for this is God's will for you in Christ Jesus."

Activity: Next time you experience a "failure," find someone to encourage in that moment, as immediately as you can. Also, find something to be happy about after it is over. Build on that. Trust me, it will change your life and the lives of those around you!

—————————————————

#11 RISE UP IN ALL WAYS ... LEGACY

Micah 6:8

"He has showed you, oh man, what is good. And what does the Lord require of you? To act justly and to love mercy and to walk humbly with your God."

In Casting Crown's song "Courageous," they dare us to fight for justice, show mercy, and demonstrate humility by relying on God and giving our lives to Him, in good times and in bad. I love the idea of a legacy. I absolutely think that we are called to live amazing legacies. However, until recently I equated this with success as much as I did living out my faith. I now believe so differently. For clarification, I absolutely believe in setting goals and striving to accomplish them. But for what purpose? It used to be for my glory (it's so easy to get caught up in personal attention in successful times), but now it is all for Him because God gave me the ability to accomplish things and my talents are a gift from Him. My gift to God is to use those talents to the best of my ability in order to glorify Him.

Hebrews 13:20–21

"May the God of peace, who through the blood of the eternal covenant brought back from the dead our Lord Jesus, that great Shepherd of the sheep, equip you with everything good for doing his will, and may he work in us what is pleasing to him, through Jesus Christ, to whom be glory for ever and ever. Amen."

Take basketball for example. To this day, I live in this truth ... being successful as a high school player and being a Division 1 scholarship athlete led me to a platform in which I could share my faith and testimony. Ultimately, it opened the door to being a coach, a mentor for young ladies. While my official role is to be a basketball coach, it is so much bigger than that. The path God put in place for me, though not straight at all times, is not a mistake. While I hope that I am a blessing to these girls, I am blessed daily by the opportunity to coach or mentor them. Legacy isn't just about the good moments, though. In fact, it's in times of adversity that people will be affected more by what we do and say. Dr. Tim Elmore, in a recent sermon at our church, said this: "Think high road, think big picture, think long term." I love this challenge. In times of conflict, think like Jesus.

2 Corinthians 4:18

"So we fix our eyes not on what is seen, but on what is unseen. For what is seen is temporary, but what is unseen is eternal."

The high road is the one less traveled. It's the one that hurts a little bit and takes effort, but keeps us from the impulsive moments and regrets. The big picture includes looking at moments as building blocks of a bigger reality. Sometimes the little battles we choose to fight are the ones that don't make a difference but do create hurt and pain. Thinking long term entails looking into the future and deciding how to react in the moment. It's understanding how the moment you are in affects those around you after today. It's taking the time to step back and think about the implications of the choice you make.

Hebrews 6:10

"God is not unjust; he will not forget your work and the love you have shown him as you have helped his people and continue to help them."

Panic at the Disco sings a song entitled "High Hopes." The lyrics encourage the listener to have high hopes and a vision to be something greater than what is "expected," in order to make a legacy. I absolutely love this song for so many reasons, but when I listen to it, I marry these lyrics with the ideas presented in the song "Only Jesus" by Casting Crowns. In this song, they argue that we aren't to leave a legacy that is our own or about us ... we are to leave a legacy in which people see and know Jesus through our life on earth. Our minister once said that a full life is a life lived for others. That's the life that God wants us to live. God gives us opportunities through our talents to make a difference, but His hope is that the difference we make is for Him. The only legacy I want to be remembered by is the legacy of living for others and for Christ, helping people find Him and His love through my actions and my words.

Romans 12:8

"If it is encouraging, let him encourage; if it is contributing to the needs of others, let him give generously; if it leadership, let him govern diligently; if it is showing mercy, let him do it cheerfully."

Activity: Do some soul searching. What is it that you want people to remember you for? What successes in this life might help you create a legacy of living for Christ and a platform to help others find their faith? Write your legacy and strive to live it out every day.

_____

#12 ENJOY THE JOURNEY

Isaiah 40:31

"But those who hope in the Lord will renew their strength. They will soar on wings like eagles; they will run and not grow weary, they will walk and not be faint."

A marathon: one of the most physically, emotionally, and mentally demanding challenges I have ever trained for and accomplished. But lost in the shuffle was the journey of that. I was so focused on the destination that I forgot to enjoy the ride and find joy in the small victories. Our first marathon was exhausting but we ran a pretty good time. The second time around came with more challenges, both during training and during the race. What it taught me was to be more appreciative of the little things. Running is something that my husband and I have done together for about twenty years. Mostly smaller road races like 5K, 10K, and half marathons. We signed up for the Disney Marathon 2015 only because we love Disney and I thought it would be amazing to run through the parks.

Colossians 2:6–7

"So then, just as you received Christ Jesus as Lord, continue to live in him, rooted and built up in him, strengthened in the faith as you were taught, and overflowing with thankfulness."

The marathon was awesome and grueling all at the same time. Just like having a baby, though, God let me forget the pain and I talked Ben into going through it all again. Four months before our second Disney Marathon, Ben started experiencing health problems. The initial concern was heart. After two trips to the hospital in an ambulance and lots of tests, it was determined that wasn't the problem. He was cleared to continue training...a blessing. The health issues continued, however, throughout training and on race day, without a pattern. He finished the race...a blessing. As we were running, I saw many runners with physical disabilities, I saw runners who had to stop due to injuries, and I remembered that I was so blessed to be healthy.

Proverbs 16:3

"Commit to the Lord whatever you do, and your plans will succeed."

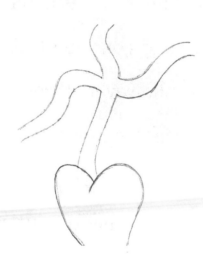

A few times during the race, I was overcome with emotion. I was reminded that things I take for granted daily are huge blessings from God and that sometimes those get lost in the shuffle of the "time" I thought I needed to get in order to feel accomplished. What did that number really mean anyway? It wasn't determining my worth. I'm already worth so much to God, we all are. The important part was the entire journey, from beginning to end, and the perseverance it took to finish the race to the best of my ability. These runs are like life in so many ways. As a mom, a wife, a teacher, and a coach there are so many times that I have placed more emphasis on the accomplishments of my students, my teams, and my family than I did on the journey that we were all on together. That is changing. It's important to set goals, give your very best to glorify Him, and then give it to God and enjoy the ride.

Philippians 1:27

"Whatever happens, conduct yourselves in a manner worthy of the gospel of Christ."

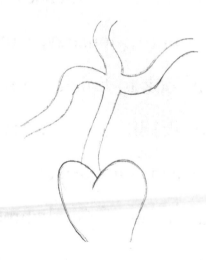

The destination, if we find success, gives us a platform. The journey is ever present, and is a huge blessing that God gives us too. It is what shapes our stories, and it is during the journey that we can make a huge impact. How we handle the journey affects us, those around us, and our final destination. Sometimes the journey is easy and sometimes it is difficult, but we can choose joy in every journey we experience because there are always blessings and God is with us all the time. One of my favorite quotes by Charles Swindoll is, "Life is 10 percent what happens to me and 90 percent how I react to it." We get to choose our attitude in the journey. The best news is that God loves us unconditionally and is equally concerned about how we handle the journey and the results of our final destination.

Romans 12:2

"Do not conform any longer to the pattern of this world, but be transformed by the renewing of your mind. Then you will be able to test and approve what God's will is-his good, pleasing, and perfect will."

Activity: For one day, slow down. Notice the world around you and take or draw pictures of what you see. Create something to help you remember that day. As an added challenge, create a goal and on your way to achieving that goal, enjoy the journey and document it well. Give yourself something to reflect back on.

_____

LOVE

#13 LIVE OUT YOUR MOTTO

Luke 10:27

"He answered, 'Love the Lord your God with all your heart and with all your soul and with all your strength and with all your mind'; and, 'Love your neighbor as yourself.'"

Find A Motto ... Or Create Your Own

"Love God, Love each other.

Plan for the future, Live in the moment.

Believe in yourself, Trust in Him."

Hebrews 11:1

"Now faith is sure of what we hope for and certain of what we do not see."

That? That is the Shappell Family Motto. It's what we try to live by. We created it; well, I did with Ben's input. It's how we want our family to live life. Loving each other doesn't just mean our family members, it means everyone we come into contact with. It's loving people well no matter what their story is. We live in the moment, not to the point of ignoring the impact on our future, but to be mindful in order to recognize God moments when they occur. We plan for the future knowing that God walks with us every moment. We carry ourselves with confidence, knowing we can do anything with God by our side and that we can trust Him to never leave.

Colossians 3:1–2

"Since, then, you have been raised with Christ, set your hearts on things above, where Christ is seated at the right hand of God. Set your minds on things above, not on earthly things."

We are not perfect and our focus does not always fall in line with this motto, but it is a goal and this shared goal gives us something to fall back on in challenging moments. Would this motto work for everyone? Absolutely not! Every person or family has to find or create their own motto. Something that reminds them of purpose and hope. Something that drives them into living more like Christ, understanding that God loves us and should be our focus always. Something that brings them back from a challenge, together with others, or simply closer to Him.

Philippians 3:14

"I press on toward the goal to win the prize for which God has called me heavenward in Christ Jesus."

This motto was a perfect one in 2014 and 2015 for sure. I missed out on watching both state softball championship games that my husband coached, the first two state softball championship games in school history. *We had a plan* in 2014... we had a trip to Hawaii already planned and, unfortunately, it was during the time the state championship would take place. The itinerary was tweaked for Ben after the Leo Lady Lions made it to the championship game, but my kids, myself, and the rest of my family carried on in Hawaii. *We lived in the moment*... I watched the game pool side on my iPad. 3A State Champions! My solitary celebration by the pool was a sight to see I'm sure. I didn't understand why things had worked out this way, but then I saw a picture of my husband praying with his team before that game... he had been given more opportunity to impact and he took full advantage to show *his love for God and for those around him.*

The very next year I was asked to be an assistant coach for the Indiana All-Star basketball team. I said yes. Then we realized it would be the same day as the state softball finals again. Not knowing what the future held for the softball team, I kept my commitment. *We believed in ourselves* and the opportunities God had provided... the games happened simultaneously in Indianapolis, in different parts of the city. I remember the tears that I cried while praying the week leading up to that Saturday and the tears I cried after I heard the final score. I had now missed both of his state championship games, and this one seemed like the one I should've been at... to comfort him at a time that they had fallen just short of a repeat. *We trusted Him*... God knew what He was doing and He wanted us to impact again, just in different sports and different parts of the city. Through our actions, our words, and the relationships we built in those moments, we are hopeful that is what we did!

1 Peter 2:9

"But you are a chosen people, a royal priesthood, a holy nation, a people belonging to God, that you may declare the praises of him who called you out of darkness into His wonderful light."

Activity: What's your motto? Take time to find one or create one and live it!

——————————————————

CLOSING

Ephesians 5:15–17

"Be very careful, then, how you live—not as unwise, but as wise, making the most of every opportunity, because the days are evil. Therefore do not be foolish, but understand what the Lord's will is."

All In:

You know that feeling when you have a goal you really want to accomplish and the last thing you really want to do is take the little steps to get there? There is that human impatience that we all possess that tells us that we can accomplish whatever we want to accomplish, but we want it to happen right now! The best example of this was training for that first marathon I spoke about earlier. Okay, 26.2 miles sounded like a lot, but I totally had this. I was "all in!" There were so many days that I didn't want to run, but we had a plan and we were going to make it happen. One thing that God has blessed me with in my personality is commitment to the task, 100 percent in, all of the time. Thankfully, Ben and I both enjoy running road races. Many times we have to train separately, but we try to run the races together. This provides a built-in accountability partner when I am struggling to be intrinsically motivated. I have always wanted to be good at what I am doing and am always harder on myself than anyone else can be on me. In fact, I am so bad about being a perfectionist at everything I pursue that I have had to learn the word "no." Still not the best at that, though, and sometimes I get pretty overwhelmed. Ben wishes I would get better at that word, because if I sign up for something it is going to be the best it can be and I will wear myself out accomplishing the task at hand. Call it high-strung, I guess. So this was my challenge. How do I jump "all in" for Jesus too?

As I mentioned before, at sixteen years old I felt that ministry tug and I would be lying if I said that was the only time in my life that the tug occurred. In fact, until I was thirty-six years old, I'm not sure that I ever felt closure on that tug. I have followed the tug a bit by working in the church in several different roles. Since college, I have filled volunteer and paid positions at church. I've been a senior high youth leader, played guitar and sang on the praise team, taught youth Sunday school, served on committees, shared my testimony at church, and directed youth camps. Outside of the church, I have worked with Youth for Christ and started a secular club called Life is Good Campaign for junior high students, which includes community service projects and ways to make the school a more positive place. I have not, however, fully committed to the church ministry. And for years I struggled with this. Was God calling me into church ministry and I was ignoring Him? That was obviously the last thing I wanted to do...ignore God. All of that was about to change.

Luke was nine years old and truly convinced that he needed to see the movie *God's Not Dead*. Since Luke has been little, he has been very into his Christian faith. He has asked a lot of questions, been very interested in church, and has found a quiet purpose in his faith in God. At one point we had him in a Sunday basketball league for five weeks and while we just attended a different church service, he had to miss Sunday school a few times. That was the first and the last time for that league. I wasn't a huge fan of Sundays being interrupted and since he didn't want to miss Sunday school, I was convinced our plans should change. We've brought our kids up the same way I was raised. Church is a routine; it happens every weekend. There is no question. It's not an argument, it is just what we do. Besides that routine and some devotions and prayer that we have done as a family, we haven't been pushy with our faith. God is the one who gets full credit for how strong our kids have always been. He has really taken hold of their hearts and led them. So when Luke first approached me with the idea of going to see *God's Not Dead*, it sounded great but I was unsure if it was age-appropriate. After much research and advice seeking, and some persistence from Luke, we decided to go. It would be life-changing for guess who? Yeah, you know.

Remember that tug that I keep referencing? Well, this movie was one of the most amazing and timely "God moments" I have ever experienced. It will forever be one of my favorite movies and I will never regret taking my Luke. There are many subplots to the movie that are very touching and if you haven't already seen it, you really must. There are so many talking points and moments of reinforcement of our faith. The main story line follows a young man who is attending a public university as a freshman. For his first assignment, he is asked to write "God is Dead" on a piece of a paper and sign it. If he fails to do this, he will fail the class. In a moment where everyone else is following the direction of the professor in order to pass, he declines. His alternative assignment is to then prove in a debate with the professor that God is NOT dead. The class will be the jury. And now you are trying to figure out why this has anything to do with me and why this would be life-changing, right?

In the midst of living an "all in" career of teaching and coaching in a public school, I had started to doubt my career. I began asking the question, was it enough? I thought maybe I wasn't doing enough for God. I was supposed to be in the church, or was I? This movie answered that question with a very convincing message and I decided that I was absolutely in the place I was supposed to be. I was in the trenches. I am an example for God in a public setting. While this comes with amazing opportunity and I was completely relieved and rejuvenated, I also now realized the amount of responsibility God had placed in my life. I knew that I would never have the opportunity to stand up in front of my classes or teams and tell them about God, but in everything I do and say, I am an example for Him and the Christian faith. This world needs church leaders, but it also needs Christians in the trenches and I was ready and willing and more motivated than ever. I was left with this question: if we were all in the battlefield at the church alone, how would we reach the unchurched, the apprehensive, the broken? Here was my ah-ha moment: in living my teaching and coaching career "all-in," I was accomplishing two things. I was using the gift God had given me to His glory and I was trying to live a Godly life in a public setting. It was like a reawakening and a redefined mission for my life. While I fall short many times, it convicted me to be so much more intentional than before. I had found my ministry.

Think About It...

What areas in your life are you "all in?"

_____

Can you think of a part of life that you are "all in" that causes conflict with your Christian faith? Could it instead be transformed into a ministry?

_____

Have you ever had an epiphany in a "God moment?" If not, keep your eyes and ears open to how He might be working in you....

_____

How can we open our hearts and minds to God's plan and to being "all in" for Him?

_____

Are you selling yourself short by questioning His plan for your "ministry" instead of embracing that He meets us where we are and works through us in many ways?

_____

What's your ministry? Or do you have more than one?

_____

How is God challenging you to live out your ministry (ministries) to the fullest?

_____

Other thoughts or reflections?

_____

_____

_____

1 Peter 4:10

"Each one should use whatever gift he has received to serve others, faithfully administering God's grace in its various forms."

Each day God gives you is an opportunity for you to live out your ministry. He provides moments for us to impact others and, if we pay attention, there is no limit to what we can do with Him by our side. Tomorrow, you may have a chance to be there for a friend, smile at someone you don't know, ask a co-worker how he or she is doing, call a family member to tell them you love them, talk to your child about his or her day, quote scripture for someone who has lost hope, listen to your spouse at the end of a busy day, show gratitude, or pray for and encourage someone who is dealing with illness or sadness. Take full advantage of every moment you are given to "show up" for someone else. Your ministry is where you are. God's plan for you is perfect. In Blanca's song "Echo," she explains that daily we are gifted 1,440 minutes and we get to decide how we are going to live those minutes. My advice? Live them out loud, showing love, grace, and patience to everyone you come into contact with ... remembering you are His hands and feet on this Earth. Every. Single. Day.

CPSIA information can be obtained
at www.ICGtesting.com
Printed in the USA
LVHW100815231119
638260LV00002B/3/P